salmonpoetry

Publishing Irish & International
Poetry Since 1981

ALSO BY NESSA O'MAHONY

POETRY
Bar Talk (iTaLiCs Press, Dublin, 1999)
Trapping a Ghost (bluechrome publishing, Bristol, 2005)
In Sight of Home (Salmon Poetry, 1999)
Her Father's Daughter (Salmon Poetry, 2014)

FICTION
The Branchman (Arlen House, 2018)

CO-EDITIONS
With Siobhan Campbell
Eavan Boland: Inside History (Arlen House, 2017)

With Paul Munden
Metamorphic: 21st century poets respond to Ovid
(Recent Work Press 2017)

The
Hollow Woman
on the Island

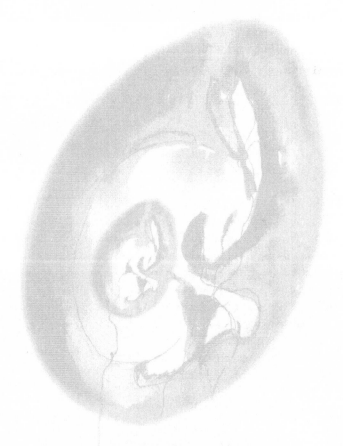

Nessa O'Mahony

Published in 2019 by
Salmon Poetry
Cliffs of Moher, County Clare, Ireland
Website: www.salmonpoetry.com
Email: info@salmonpoetry.com

ISBN 978-1-912561-63-6

Cover Artwork: *"Generational Form" by Kim Sharkey*
Cover Design & Typesetting: *Siobhán Hutson*

Printed in Ireland by Sprint Print

*Salmon Poetry gratefully acknowledges the support of
The Arts Council / An Chomhairle Ealaíon*

for Peter Salisbury

Contents

I

II

III

I

Bogeyman

1st March 1965

When I was one they resurrected him,
dug up the scraps of bone from Pentonville quicklime,
packed them in oak, draped flags, slow-marched
the gun-carriage through sleety 60s streets.

Snow-flickered images on our TV screens,
huddled crowds signing as the carriage passed
to the beat of Charles Mitchell's sonorous tones
requiem in pacem.

Did it come from this, that first terror?
Did I confuse Casement with the Michan's Mummy,
think his Glasnevin tomb must be visited,
a crusty hand shaken?

Was it he who made shadows darken
on the landing, exert a gravitational pull
through the door of the upstairs bedroom,
towards the wardrobe where the bogeyman hid

till displaced by whatever fear *du jour*
gripped me bonily?
In the 70s it was 'Tubular Bells'
that lowered temperatures, raised sheets.

In the 80s it was whatever blood carried
illicit through veins and dangerous apertures.
Each decade found its own vortex
of imps straddling chests, white mares snorting.

It ends with the banality of a waiting room:
a dead celebrity waving from the cover of an old *Hello*,
a raised bump beneath skin, a white-draped man
scanning penumbras on illuminated screens.

A Vertebra in Slow Time

for Geraldine Mitchell

It could be
a Henry Moore,
propped by the door
in sun-bleached calcium.
Mossed saddle
emerald-bright,
topmost point
of its tricorn
casts shadow
on the plastered wall.
The ovoid gape
where the spinal chord
once ran
is a perfect eye
of whatever storm
beached it.
No living memory
recalls who found it,
dragged it up
from the shore,
and placed it in lieu
of a boot-scrape
perhaps,
a hiding place
for keys.
Still useful
all these centuries
later, calcified into art.

Simple Arithmetic of the Human Egg

Born
with two
million but the
maths are insane. Three
quarters are gone by 13; lose
1,000 more each month the next
40 years until nothing: a huge spheroid
blank where posterity used to be. I might look
just the same, *who the hell is she kidding*, don't walk
with a slight limp and I don't float into air because
this new weightlessness can't tether me. I have
new tastes: for omelettes, sunny-side ups,
for Fabergé, old Hitchcock flicks, ex-
ceptional puns *don't start m*e,
for pebbles washed up,
edge wavepolished
into Henry
Moore.

Folk Memory

No stone marks the spot.
No crucifix in a field
no greener than most.
The odd rock, cattle-kicked,
is all that marks a heifer's path
through gates, bars rusted
and bent, the lock shot.

The grass grows the same here:
the odd blown-in
pollinated by cloven hooves.
We keep our mouths shut,
look the other way
as we file up the road to Mass,
and quell an impulse to sign the cross
when we skirt the wall.

O'Leary's Grave

They're reshooting the Rising
up at Collins Barracks.
White Winnebagos line up.
Volunteers form an orderly queue
for the catering, Asgard safely
moored behind cordons.

They'll get it in higher definition
this time, take all the takes
they need, apply the make-up
to Pearse's squint expertly,
photoshop Dev in
if the director requires.

Extras lounge about,
drift in and out of colonnades,
wander further afield,
tall skinnies in hand.

Out front, Croppy's Acre is padlocked.
The Corpo turned the key
when the citizens started
bedding down there, sharing
sleeping bags and needles,
messing up the view.

Right now, two of them frisk a third
who hasn't moved for hours:
still-life, ready
for his close-up.
Zoom in to Romantic Ireland
blue-inked on his wrist.

Age Shall Not Weary Them

in memory of Private Michael Walsh, 24/10/1918

St. Enda's in its prime; sky clear, air crisp,
the sheddings of beech in piles
where the park warden swept them.
'Brown gold,' he smiles, undaunted
at a task made futile by the next gust.
We talk of public affairs; a presidential poll,
one candidate leading the field.
'He's 77,' he shakes his head.

I think of my mother, all of 90,
packing her bag today for a foreign trip,
to pay respects to a man she never met,
who died a decade before her birth,
peppered by shrapnel in a trench
on the French-Luxembourg border.

She'll visit his white-crossed grave,
plant a marker, a poppy perhaps,
with her daughter and a scattering
of cousins from both sides of the Atlantic.
She'll say a prayer, a poem,
cast a glance over row upon row
of white marble, tree-enclosed.

We shall not forget, how could we?
Shared genes give the same nose,
domed head, the pale blue eyes
that measure you up in an instant.
An instant was all it took
for Private Walsh, at 30 years old.
The cemetery will be swept,
poplars shedding tears
on the living, on the dead
of the Meuse-Argonne.

From a Beachcomber's Manual

On reading that Irish students are asked
to abandon arts for 'stem' subjects

Nacre is the noun
for the iridescent inner lining
of bivalves and molluscs;
nacreous, the adjective.
Don't worry how that sounds:
no matter that it whiffs
more of the grave
than of the milky prism
of creams, blues
glistening as the tide recedes
through bladderwrack.

Dreamers gave us mother of pearl
and you know what trouble
dreams got us into.
Stick to the facts,
google if unsure.
And for reason's sake
don't make things up;
metaphors are obsolete
these post-factual days.

Absence

Our regular route: across the bridge,
up the hill, past trees,
along neat green squares
that front each suburban house.
Station wagons, sentinel
at each gate for a dog sniff,
a twitch of curtains.
But no-one looks out
at this empty sky, bereft
of clouds, of movement.
Was it last year
that swifts carved their curve
here? Or the year before?
The nest on the burglar alarm
has crumbled, a winter's storm
washed away any other trace,
like the names of things
we knew only yesterday.

'And the soul creeps out of the tree'....

at Annaghmakerrig reading Louise Glück and John Berryman

the way out, a c-section of exposed bark
where the feller swung his axe
too wildly for neatness.
Now here and there
along the lake's reed shore
are stumps like so many molars.

No trace of the famed view
that launched a thousand haikus.
The wind lifts;
the balcony door shifts
wide enough to ask us
if red still matters,
regardless of wheelbarrow function.

Two desks, two chairs;
one writes, one taps sweet
nothings: nothing sweet here.

Sniper Alley

looks nothing like the one they warned of
in the days when threats were shadows
cast by a neighbour's firs on the back lane.
We obeyed curfew, paused kick-the-can
at dinner time, withdrew to gardens,
waited it out until morning or when old enough
to risk it without older sister or brother.

We didn't know then that danger doesn't lurk
behind the pole or ESB transformer;
it hides in full-view, prescription in hand,
as we gaze device-rapt, scroll or flick
through images of our younger selves,
lining up each click of the telescopic sight.

Mrs Pass If You Can

My father named you that,
after an old Cork presence
from childhood,
and it captured your stance,
alert, close at the gate,
attuned to a wind's shift,
the neighbours' arrivals, departures,
the weight of a shopping bag, its clink
and what that might mean.

You brought the old ways –
the chat after the mart,
the glance out of a half door –
to a suburban street
where children colonised the road
and mothers pruned branches
when freed from kitchen stoves.

Time passed in that devious blink;
you withdrew, closed the gate,
kept the doors and windows shut,
made a phone-call next door
rather than risk the shop.
Until the day came when
a crammed letter box
gave its own intelligence.

The for sale sign will go up.
Somebody else will the pave the front,
paint the front door,
let strangers pass as they may.

Do Not Ask

in memory of Philip Casey, 4th February 2018

We didn't plan for it,
but these past days
we've stalked death,
as we wandered streets,
looked up at domes,
tried to remember the past
without googling it.

Skulls everywhere:
on market stalls,
behind glass in the ritz
of Burlington arcade,
bells tolling the footfall.

Then the pink room,
where Keats spotted red,
signed his death warrant
in a four-poster bed.

And here, now, returned
to our borrowed bed
in the shades of St. Pauls,
we take our beat
from the chimes,
till the phone beeps
with the news.

You'd have seen the joke;
were always the first
to try out new technology,
to match it to old words.

Another bell:
and I know
for whom it tolled,
old friend.

A Poppy for Aoife

for the Beary family

That was the summer
we had to learn patience,
follow the garden's rules
and trust the slow-mo reveal
as each green pod plumped
and split its seams,
letting red silk out.

Breath held, we'd watch
the skies; one downpour
would tear those skirts,
trample the soil
with petals.
But the weather held,
the sky heavy as our thoughts.

Take your time:
your parents waited
all their lives for you,
like their parents, too.

April Hawthorn

i.m. Susan Cox

Hedgerows scant, late Spring hangs on bare branches, buds
too tender-pink for the wind's rough trade, the weight of
rain. I stand and watch droplets lined up as if waiting for
something. Odd that you never see them form, detach, fall
into unknowing. They outstare the watcher: I move on.
Another month and you would have seen boundaries
blossom, the verge defined by froth. Mayflower softens the
blow, escorting bystanders from this world to the next.

A single white rose.
Drapes close as Ferrier sings
What is life without…

The Hare on the Chest

in memory of Josie Grey

A regular from your repertoire:
a man walks into a field,
watches a pack, their baying,
the zig-zag chase of a breathless hare,
its desperate leap of faith into the dark
gap between the man's coat and chest.
How he feels its heart beat, holds his ground
as the hounds surge.

The crowd now follows your coffin,
edges down the incline towards
Ballindoon Abbey, pauses to look west
as low cloud rolls over the water
and the lake's own breath is exhaled.
There are murmurs: family well-met,
old friends remembered, enmities forgot.
You're laid to rest, snug on the hare's chest.

II

The Hollow Woman Waits

The soon to be hollow woman waits
in a room with four doors, all closed,
whose opening stops the heart, restarts
it arythmically.

It is the day for a-words;
soon she will grapple a new one –
tossed by the man with the screen
turned towards him, eyes turned out
at her like lasers he won't be using
if it comes to the cut.

She still prays it won't
but now her body is against her,
learning the script of what she's read
on websites, with illustrations –
butcher's cuts
of possibility.

Each twinge another knot
in the noose she's weaving herself.
She looks at the pile of glossies
from two years ago and picks one up;
old news is better
than new news
when you have to wait
in a room with four doors,
none of them open, yet.

II

One word, three syllables:
Atypia.
It is pronounced cautiously
by the white-coat uncertain
if the patient response
will be a stereotype
– gasp, sob, stagger.

She grasps
at uncertainty,
though that life-line
seems suddenly shorter
than it did 30 minutes ago.

He mentions further consults.
She nods and tries to banish the thought
of balding men swapping slides
over glasses of port,
white coats well-laundered
of blood spots.

Once home, bravado returned,
the urge to google is ignored
till the eleventh hour has struck.

The Hollow Woman on the Island

The hollow woman sits in her car
watching the sea lick its lips
at the edge of the pier.
till the sides of the car disappear
and the windscreen dissolves
into waves and grey crests
drawing her into depths
she has dreamed of nightly.
She does not float ,
(despite the vacuum inside her)
        she rolls.
Edges rounded off
by the water's oscillation
till she's smooth, buffed
into ovoid shape,
tide-tossed onto damp sand
to be plucked up,
pocketed, placed with care
on a mantlepiece, a grave-top.

The Hollow Woman at Bohea

The stone tells you
to follow the pilgrim path
though the route may spiral,
the grass track taking you
mountain-wards
might pivot back
into trees and mossy brooks.

It tells you to listen;
the fork in the unmarked road
is the very place
the cuckoo calls.

The stone tells you notice
every cup-marked drop
in the hazel-dappled light:
if baptismal, burial, dew
it doesn't matter.

Each key-hole cut into rock
holds deeper than the cross
incised by those who'd claim
the slopes and the sun's descent.

What matter
if the eye of faith betrays?
Trace your truth
with a thumb, a tongue,
an index finger,
a thought,

a scratch
on paper.

The Hollow Woman Reflects on the Illusion of Abundance

Yesterday, the garden
sounds were tickertape:
two parent wrens
cordoning a fledge
as it careered
from hedge to vine
and back again,
settling on the slant
of the garden shed.

Oblivious, it seemed,
to the one for sorrow
creasing the air
for sharkbait,
to the hollow woman,
raising her fist at it,
Dora Trottwood-like,
forgetful for once
of the rogue cells
multiplying.

III

"In Ainm Croim".

Macha na bó, Chorca Dhuibhne, August 2016

We never knew what those words meant,
and we ducked when we heard them.
You never explained sounds
handed-down the generations;
exasperation planted in the DNA
by North Cork ancestors
who incursed into Corca Dhuibhne,
came back with that linguistic stick of rock.

I think of it now as I walk what might be
the same pathway your forefather took,
trodden for millennia through skutch-grass,
the vertiginous slopes of hills
where sheep perch oblivious,
where cows pastured their way into name-place,
where the self-same Crom was born.

The path leads on, the hills get steeper.
Remains of walls are all that's left
of Driscolls and Dinneens.
The last of them served cake to travellers;
light relief from wind and falling stones
and memories of going Winter-mad
when the mist descended and stayed,
lacing the valley floor with droplets.

Black dog, black moods, black God
at the point where valleys end,
where waterfalls flow upwards.

Mantra

Your brother came often those last weeks,
a limber version of you,
a reminder of what might have been
had illness gone elsewhere.

He was convinced
the right arrangement of words
might see you through,
a practice each night before sleep
to imprint subconscious belief
with recovery.

I didn't dare catch your eye,
the most articulate part
now the swallow was gone and the lips
refused to shape syllables in the right order.
An eye that could do fury, impatience, love
in quick succession.
But this time you nodded,
index finger graciously pointing
that visiting hours were up.

Seeing my uncle out,
I promised to do my best
to persuade the recusant,
remembering how your words
would help my passage into sleep.

Last thing each night,
you'd perch on the bed ,
fold my hands in prayer
as I followed your lead:

Hello Holy God this is Nessa speaking,
God bless me and make me very good.
God bless my Mam and Dad,
and all my friends and relations, living and dead,
particularly my Granny in Cork,
and my Granny in Ballinasloe, and my Granddad.

The rhythm has stayed with me
40 years and more,
easing the wait in the dark,
forming my soul's belief
in the pattern of sounds.

First Christmas

in memory of Trude Salisbury

From the photograph it is clear
she had never known joy like this,
taking you in her arms those first weeks,
bundling you tighter than the few things
stowed for the journey.

England looked nothing like Wien,
the hard stares that could surprise
even years later: her accent
a trigger for those who didn't care
she'd spent the time hiding.

She came in search of a father,
found instead a man I never met
save in the softness of your eyes,
your quiet smile. And she promised
that Christmas, the first as a family,

would be the best one yet.
Did she scour the whole of Chester
to find the flour, ground almond,
exotic spices, to make Oma's
Linzer Kuchen from scratch?

Your brother found the recipe
in a drawer. You'll try it this year,
relying on words on the page,
though the voice you still hear
may remind you how to measure it.

At Masada

If I were to remember you anywhere
it would be here, cliff-top,
59 metres above Dead Sea-level,
seated on rock, light bouncing off
the white glare of your sun-hat,
breath spasming in your 85th year
of brooking no obstacles.
We heard the history
on the way up: the no surrender,
the 960 men, women and children
opting for glorious death. You opt
for glorious life, gasp the thin air
left in your body, grasp the chance
to rise, resume the tour, run upstream
of tourists swarming the citadel.

Holy Land

for my pilgrim mother

Faith might be easier
if it was simply a matter
of almond blossom,
of blood anemones
spotting the hillside,
or the diamond blue
of lupins and violets
along the valley
still called Armageddon.

Prayer might come quicker
if the caves stayed unbuilt-upon,
if layer on layer of
begun by Byzantines,
destroyed by Persians,
rebuilt by Crusaders,
destroyed by Muslims,
of twentieth century wars
remained scattered dust
in the Samarian wilderness.

Abraham does his best,
yellow baseball cap at a tilt
to beacon us on through traders
and treacherous steps,
where nothing is as
the guidebook describes it.

The tears come,
unsurprisingly, not on
the Via Dolorosa
or the slow sepulchral crawl
past Calvary, the quick shove
through the tomb

but in a quiet place:
a vaulted roof
of white Jerusalem stone,
where a smiling,
West Cork Franciscan
guards the door,
where steps descend
to the cave your namesake
may have been born in,

where the notes soar as we gather
a rag-tag choir at St. Ann's altar:

oh sacrament most holy
oh sacrament divine

and I join in,
try descant
to my mother's alto tones,
find harmonies
I've practised all my life,
that I came all these miles to sing.

Cross-Channel Auntie

I wasn't expecting you to answer the phone.
You're home alone and I'm blaming
cross-channel noise
for your new voice, your adult poise
and I'm thinking that any moment now
we'll be talking about make-up and diets
and godforbid boyfriends, the whats, the whos.

My throat dries with the screech of time
full-throttling past babygros and barbies,
spangled eyelids and french plaits,
past first communion whites,
improbable loves for St Pats,
or Leeds United,
first dances, best friends
interchangeable, augmented

and there's no stopping
this screaming train
of don't do what I dids,
or didn't do or should have done
or could have done if only
and what next and
will you come visit me
in the Home?

I pull the emergency cord.
'Tell Mammy I called, won't you?"

Epithalamium

for Catherine O'Mahony and James Coffey, 2nd June 2018

Contracting universe? A conjurer's trick?
How else to explain that one minute
you're on my lap, tearful, redfaced,
distracted by shreds of tissue
littering your granny's dressing table,
the next you're gliding down the aisle,
confetti-led, golden, elegant, and I'm the one
tearing shreds off hankies, dabbing an eye.

Time plays particular tricks:
the then and now upends us, double vision
blurs and we swallow our gasps
that the next generation is taller, shinier,
lovelier than we could ever have dreamed of
when we were the stars of our own imaginings.

So take it on trust, dear girl of the hour,
that when the time comes, I'll gladly take hold
of a tearful, questioning bundle
of outrage, dandle her on my lap,
build the hankie shreds higher till the pile erupts
and I hear her mother's echo in her laugh.

The King of Britain's Daughter

for Peter

They have reversed that old tale.
In theirs, the Irish girl returns
with the son of Britain,
makes a new home out of old bolt-holes,
keeps an eye, when she remembers to,
that his quiet ways don't shelter sadness,
and he doesn't take to watching skies
for starlings from home.

They have faced the rage of the Irish Sea,
walked the welcoming warmth of city walls
built on sandstone,
buried parents on either side of the pond.
They've returned each time, she convinced
that her love of Wicklow hills
would tether them both.

They both walk the strand,
beach-comb, pick up messages
they encode for each other.
Does it matter what bird says your name,
or which coast it flies from?

Super Moon on the M6

All dusk it was glare;
oncoming headlights flaring
over the median,
world tunnelling light
to the grey verge,
dented tin sides
of lorries slow-laning,
hemming me in
as I left the sun behind.

Then a disc so bright
it made me laugh out loud
when I recognised her,
my knuckles wheel-clenched,
after so many miles
of straight lines.

She was rising
like a parachute in reverse
when I set myself homeward,
arcing over flatlands,
bogs, towns, silhouettes.

The Shannon crossed,
outline of swans
were like shades of the past
I couldn't wait for.

She might have filled the sky,
so pink her intention,
so inflated her will, and so strong
her pull the road curved
away from her.

Morning on Montpelier

Then there is the morning
when the view of the Mournes
is a gift, strafing the horizon
like a Shangri La north of Dublin

with its saucer bay,
tauter than plastic
where toy ferries ply their trade
to all points east.

No matter that a front
approaches stealthily,
that this crisp dry air
will moisten again, the wind pick up;
that in Kilmashogue cemetery
the slabs will re-arrange
yet again and spell out
the word of the season.

For this moment, at least,
mud pools are diamante,
a jay flutes through conifers,
a crow's signature flourishes in air.

Air Accident, Brookwood

All week long the spectacle;
aerial acrobats of every size and hue,
skills deployed with the *brio*
of innocence over experience
among clematis vines and bamboo.

This morning a blue tit,
rotating on a wind chime,
one wing extended,
Barnum & Bailey-style.

I admire the grace,
the increasing speed,
then register
the not quite rightness,
the frantic quality
as the bird pecks the chime.

It quietens as I approach,
the weighted string wrapped tight
around the extended wing,
cutting to sinew.
I try to loosen the tie
as it pecks, its claws
gnarled on the pendulum
my leaden fingers fumble.

I retreat, seek out
the smallest blade I can find,
picture the panicked rise and fall
of that feathered chest.

When I return, all is as was,
the wind chime stilled,
the tree empty,
not even a yellow feather
floating in the air.

Two Encounters with the *Lutra lutra*:

I

At the rise of a climbing road
through fields and Mayo coast.
We've entered Clare Abbey en masse,
heard verse and chapter, admired
the O'Malley grasp of the theatrical.
Look upwards, vaulted ceiling
criss-crossed by painted beams,
between them russet scenes
of men with spears, of cockerels.

Others see a hound but I claim
an unmistakable serpentine back,
its long, tapering tale
and imagine a pirate's delight
as it sinews in and out
of rock pools, gape filled
with pieces of eight.

II

When sight follows thought
on a Saturday walk by the Dodder.
We are stopped by a splash,
the glint of fish in her mouth;
we cannot keep up
with the speed of the sleek
turns as the river crests the weir
and we fumble with ways
not to forget. *Just watch*.

She scales with ease the ford
six times her height,
twists and turns
towards the reeds,
her rippling wake
decreasing the circle
to infinity.

Timoleague

at the Franciscan Abbey, West Cork

They have graves too,
wings spanned where they've fallen,
holy ghosts of pigeon and dove
in a mottled mess, placed out of view,
or drawn here, below ground,
to the cool damp of old stone,
the window shafting light from the estuary.

Bolus Head Sonata

Unlikely looking gift, this five-barred,
metal gate, rusting, crossed,
tethered in its lock by blue nylon strings.
The signs unwelcoming: dogs beware,
walkers climb at their peril
in this kingdom of scrub and rock.

But if you hold your ground,
if the wind is in the right direction,
the gate will sing to you,
notes seemingly haphazard
unless you wait for a pattern.

doh soh fah doh
lah soh fah doh

Contrapuntal recitative, hollow,
a blast of close encounters,
than a lull so long
you think you have imagined it
until it begins again, the same lilt,
the same scaling heights,
a luthier's delight.

A chough breaks in,
his bass notes have no role
in this tubular belling
as it funnels wind,
revolves it into tune again

and again

and again.

Lady Chapel

Ely Cathedral, 1541

They enter blinking,
light blinding after slender aisles
and vaulting arches
that drew their eyes upwards
to the octagon heart of stone.
They hesitate, recollecting
the urge to bow down
in this tall pale square,
windows without stain.

They are crowded by carved figures,
knights, saints, pious ladies,
holy glances downcast,
peasants at their tasks, equestrian lords.
Above the altar at the centre wall,
a demure Virgin fools nobody.

At first, a few half-hearted swipes,
but plaster cuts fast, their chisels
slicing like knives through lard
and the heat catches, igniting them,
murmurs rising to roars,
arms striking out in all directions,
cuffing their neighbours.
Soon the tiled floor
disappears under white debris,
fragments of face, an ear, a nose.
Not one missed, no cherub left uncut,

Heads and shoulders white,
they draw back, panting,
mop their brows
and observe their handiwork,
sweat etching lines
into the wide smile of the Green Man.

Alcmene's dream

(after Ovid's *Metamorphoses Book IX* L205–326)

I dreamt I had a son:
a chubby, dimpled child
whose blurry eyes shut
as he fixed on my breast
and sucked life from me.

I gave it gladly. Nobody spoke
of the spite that midwifed me,
the servant love that freed.

Men told of twelve labours;
what did they know of seven days,
of seven nights pushing a hero,
cell by cell, out into history?

I woke to a dusty corner
where a cradle might have stood.

The Myth Kitty

for Siobhán Campbell

The myth kitty purrs,
a perfect ginger curl
in the slanting rays of equinox.
Whiskers twitch and orange
talons flex each time a poet,
bored, takes out his Homer,
strokes Achilles' sword,
transforms some innocent
into wood or sound or quarry.

Her tail flicks away
every stolen child,
each mother in pursuit,
those vengeful wives
jealous of pulchritude.
She arches, sighs,
ignores that fact
is scratching at the door.

Orphan

This much we knew in 1968:
'Home' was a mam and dad,
a couch and semi-d, a car and a crew
of scruffy brothers and sisters
piled in to the Austin
for day-trips or visits
to towns with narrow streets
and grey-cottaged terraces.

'The home' was something else,
pronounced differently, a whisper
of knowledge shared with a grown-up's
glance over cups of tea.
Which was all we needed to see
that the girl in the baggy skirt
and woollen tights was contraband,
that we should be polite when we barred
her from games of tag or kick the can.

She was walking Original Sin
thought we didn't know yet
about scarlet letters or magdalenes
or concrete crypts for the bad seed,
the rotten apples, the jargon applied
when sorting wheat from the chaff.
We didn't look over walls inscribed with a cross;
our charity began at home, and ended there.

Diaspora

His regular spot
was back to the wall,
curled foetus-tight,
at the end of the canal,
near the bridge
at Baggot Street,

a paper cup beneath his chin -
but no buttercup glow
unless from 50 cents
someone dropped in.

"Change, spare change,"
may be the only words
he knows in the mother tongue
of those who pass,
who stop at the kiosk
for a *latte grande*.

I fish a coin out, fair exchange
for the information I seek.
He cannot read my lips,
pushes back the tip
of his scraggy wool cap.

I repeat;
his faces lights up
as he pronounces *'Bosnia'*
as if the syllables
were a sweet on his tongue

in the November hoar
of a Dublin morning,
his brave new world
passing by.

Writer's Retreat

The farmer who strides onto an empty field
has more plot than me; there's time
to count his steps, to guess the measure
of him, as he assesses gaps in hedging,
checks the ewes, conducts the cows to their feet
in an orchestrated wave of movement.

One, dreaming legends of *toro*, stands her ground,
goes her own course till a brandished stick
copy-edits it better than she can.
Sounds off and out of view;
the leaves wind-shift
suggests a chance denouement
until a sudden breaker in the bay
asserts its own falling action.

To My Dear Biographer

from Mary Wollstonecraft to William Godwin

No man knew me better, or treated me
more as equal in heart and intellect.
We forged our own society, late, it's true,
and would have endured after all the false beginnings,
the moments when an end seemed
the only outcome to my Werther wanderings.

I chose death, but death, it seems,
could bide its time. Until then,
you were the bridge where I could leap
to the depths of an untroubled sleep,
a waking to warmth. A golden age
that lasted eighteen months.

Did you forget, then, in those first few weeks,
shutting out the world,
poring over drafts, food trays piling up,
pausing only to refill a glass,
sharpen the tallow wick,
as the ink flowed, word upon word?

Didn't you recall the Tønsberg church,
the dusty crypt where life
was petrified into remembrance?
Treasons against humanity, I said.
Did you really want my corpse preserved,
my sins etched out on the embalmer's plate?

Brown Veneer Benches

after Patrick Kavanagh

O brown veneer benches of Belfield,
the light of my dreams you thieved,
you blunted the blade of ambition,
left only notions received.

Your priests black-robed and chalky,
their spectacles cathode-gleamed
as they chanted the latest male deity,
deconstructed every text and theme.

We watched each newly appointed,
each successor, each fresh son and heir
as they queued for their tutor confession
down the beige Block J corridor.

We dutiful vestal virgins
wrapped blue yellow scarves to our chest,
scoured library shelves for sisters,
felt the lake's chill wind instead.

It took me another decade
to put your lessons aside,
to forget every notion of canon
and go along for the ride

with every great woman writer
who waited (in vain) to be heard,
with the chorus of Paddy and Eavan,
not male, not female, just word.

Opening at the Centre Culturelle

Her flat shoes draw me to small talk.
She stands by the writer's sculpted head,
hair perfect, scarf Hepburnesque
as she balances her canapé and vin blanc.

She came in '65 and never left,
was in and out of work, taught, fashion-designed,
knew Jean Michel Jarre before the fame,
lost touch with home in the late '70s.

She doesn't get out much now,
just the odd opening
when the wine flows
and the old crowd emerges

from apartments in Neuilly sur Seine
to raise the flag in Rue des Irlandais.
All this in rapid monotone, mascara lids
unblinking as she weighs my prospects.

Conversation dies. I eye her ring
– a mount of white gold with one pearl –
as a prelude to escape.

"Try it on," she says.
Seeing no way to refuse,
I slip the cold band on my finger.

Mollie Remembers It Well

Paris 1922

By then it was too late;
the books unwrapped, stacked
blue-front top on the table
set up by that old boot
to catch the light
off Rue de l'Odéon.

She barely let me touch
the precious horde; didn't care
that Jem had bored me for years
with it, droning the words off,
striding through rooms in Trieste,
more Paris flats than
you could shake a stick at.

I should be writing the book
on midnight flits,
on looking the other way
when the grocer refused,
on queuing for discards
as the marché closed:
ten lettuces for a franc.

So I didn't have the heart
when he arrived in state,
cigar clamped, his life
beginning at 40,
to mention the date.
Such a small thing to forget:
we kissed first
on the 17th.

Bloomsday 2004

Not snot-green, today,
and sixty miles away
though if I close my eyes
I can reel
a straight line
to link this
seaside Britishness
of strolls and ice-cream cones
and white-haired revellers
with Martello towers,
stiff winds,
unpulchritudinous flesh
bobbing.

If Homer Came to Iveragh …

She would go up the hill at Bolus,
pass the gape of ruined cottages,
tip the wink to fellow travellers
labouring in each artist's cell.
She'd doff a cap to Séan Ó Conaill's shade
leaning sunrise-side of the Teach Seanachái,
reciting Archbishop MacHale's tale of Troy.

She'd climb further,
watch the sea, not wine-dark today,
but quick-silver, glinting cloud-clefts;
she would observe the stones in the fields
assembling themselves into pattern.
She'd stop here, ford the fence,
gaze on simple slate, cross-inscribed,
guarding the collapsed Oratory.

She'd remember that prayer starts
in the same place as story:
where the mind stills long enough
to hear sea crashing on rock,
to learn each note of the chough's cough,
how they banter on fence-staves.

She'd watch the young farmer herd,
his lips moving to learn the words
of a tale he'd heard somewhere,
spreading his hands out in emphasis
as his captive audience chews.

And she would know that story starts
where each knot of barbed wired
links phrase to phrase,
chair to chair of the listeners
circled in rooms, round fires,
gazing at the face of the teller,
watching her words shape, her phrases
transform the girl with the capán draíocht
as she makes her way home to the Aegean.

Cill Rialaig 25th October 2016

Acknowledgments

I'm grateful to the editors of the following anthologies, broadcasters, magazines and journals where some of these poems first appeared:

Amethyst Review, Backstory online journal, Banshee Lit, Coast to Coast to Coast, Honest Ulsterman, Metamorphic: 21st century poets respond to Ovid, Poetry Ireland Review, Poetry Jukebox, Rattalpax, Reading The Future, RTE's Lyric File, RTE's *The Poetry Programme, The Enchanting Verses Literary Review, The Green Lea Down, The Irish Times, The Pickled Body, The Poet's Quest for God, The Stinging Fly, The Trees of Kilbroney Park, The Well Review, Washing Windows?, Ygdragsil.*

I owe a deep debt of gratitude to An Chomhairle Ealaíon / The Arts Council for a literature bursary that bought me the necessary time and space to complete this collection. Thanks too to Cill Rialaig and the Irish Writers Centre for the residency in 2016 where some of these poems were written.

Thanks to Tess Gallagher for her friendship and support. Very special thanks for Paul Maddern for his astute reading of the manuscript and the wise counsel he offered. Thanks, too, to Damian Smyth for some very good advice at a key moment and to Maeve O'Sullivan for her advice on haibun. I'm grateful too to Mary O'Donnell, Jean O'Brien, Arthur Broomfield, Selese Roche, Donald Gardner, Brid Connolly, Neil Donnelly and Clare O'Reilly for their suggestions on individual poems.

NESSA O'MAHONY was born in Dublin and lives in Rathfarnham where she works as a freelance teacher and writer of poetry and fiction. She was awarded an Arts Council of Ireland literature bursary in 2004, 2011 and 2018, a Simba Gill Fellowship in 2005 and an artists' bursary from South Dublin County Council in 2007. She has published four volumes of poetry, edited and co-edited anthologies and has co-edited a book of criticism on the work of Eavan Boland. She also writes crime fiction. She presents The Attic Sessions, a literary podcast, which she produces with her husband, Peter Salisbury.

salmonpoetry

Cliffs of Moher, County Clare, Ireland

"Like the sea-run Steelhead salmon that thrashes upstream to its spawning ground, then instead of dying, returns to the sea – Salmon Poetry Press brings precious cargo to both Ireland and America in the poetry it publishes, then carries that select work to its readership against incalculable odds."

TESS GALLAGHER

The Salmon Bookshop
& Literary Centre

Ennistymon, County Clare, Ireland

Listed in *The Irish Times'* 35 Best Independent Bookshops